Dedicated in friendship to Dick and Monica Coles

First Book of Bassoon Solos

by

LYNDON HILLING

and

WALTER BERGMANN

Faber Music Limited

London

Bärenreiter-Verlag, Kassel : *Boosey & Hawkes (Australia) Pty Ltd, Sydney*
Boosey & Hawkes (Canada) Ltd, Willowdale : *G. Schirmer Inc, New York*

© 1979 by Faber Music Ltd
First published in 1979 by Faber Music Ltd
3 Queen Square London WC1N 3AU
Music drawn by Michael Terry
Cover design by Shirley Tucker
Printed in England by Halstan & Co Ltd

Contents

Preface

This book will provide the beginner on the bassoon with a repertoire of solos playable from the very first lesson. It is hoped that it will also offer a variety of pieces in contrasting styles which can be enjoyed for their musical merit and enable the player to explore the expressive potential of the instrument.

The pieces have been graded according to finger technique.

Though the piano parts have been kept as simple as possible the journeyman pianist is well advised to prepare them carefully so that the piano fully complements the bassoon.

Short explanatory notes have been provided for each piece.

The authors would like to thank Malcolm Tyler for his invaluable advice and assistance in the preparation of this book.

LYNDON HILLING

WALTER BERGMANN

1. Ostinato

W.B.

2. Yugoslav Dance

Traditional

Da Capo al FINE

2

3. Polka

Czech Traditional

4. Czech Dance

Traditional

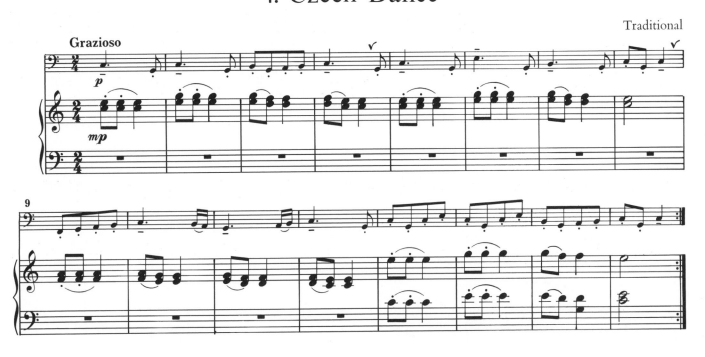

5. Barcarolle

L.H.

6. Variations on a German Christmas Song

W.B.

7. Gavotte

JACQUES AUBERT
(1689–1753)

8. Romance

W.B.

9. Menuet du Tambourin

JACQUES HOTTETERRE (Le Romain)
(c. 1680–1761)

10. Minka

Russian Folksong

11. Passacaglia

12. Duet

W.B.

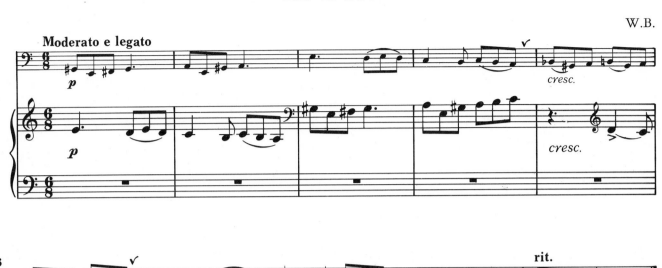

13. Hymn

JOHANN SEBASTIAN BACH
(1685–1750)

13

14. Waltz

FRANZ SCHUBERT
(1797–1828)

15. Minuet

HENRY PURCELL
(1659–1695)

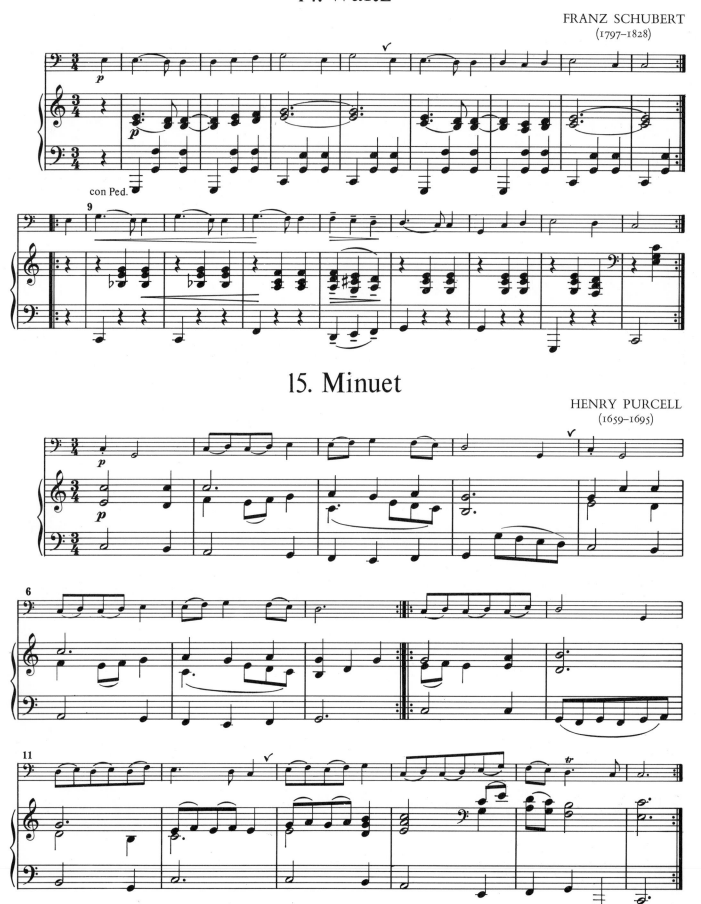

16. Andante

FRANZ SCHUBERT
(1797–1828)

17. Nobody's Jigg

English Country Dance
(1721)

18. Jig

HENRY PURCELL
(1659–1695)

19. Cockle - Shells

English Country Dance
(1721)

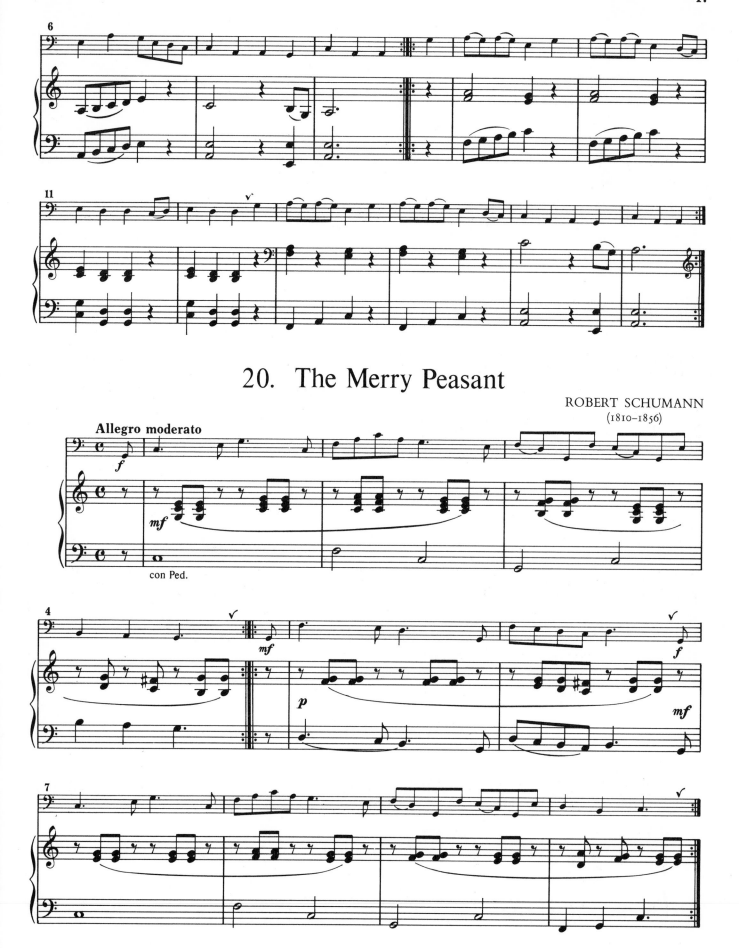

20. The Merry Peasant

ROBERT SCHUMANN
(1810–1856)

21. Song

PHILIP ROSSETER
(1568–1623)

22. Welsh Folk Song I

Traditional

23. Gavotte

FRANCESCO BARSANTI
(c. 1690–1772)

24. Welsh Folk Song II

Traditional

25. Prelude

JOHANN SEBASTIAN BACH
(1685–1750)

26. Ländler

FRANZ SCHUBERT
(1797–1828)

27. Rustic March

CARL MARIA VON WEBER
(1786–1826)

28. Duo

GEORG PHILIPP TELEMANN
(1681–1767)